j920 A545t
Tad Lincoln's restless wriggle
:pandemonium and patience in
the President's house /
Anderson, Beth,

JAN 1 2 2022

D0461587

TAD LINCOLN'S
Pandemonium and Patience
RESTLESS WRIGGLE
in the President's House

BETH ANDERSON   Illustrated by S. D. SCHINDLER

CALKINS CREEK
AN IMPRINT OF BOYDS MILLS & KANE
New York

I don't know but I may succeed in governing the nation, but I do believe I shall fail in ruling my own household.

—Abraham Lincoln

Thomas Lincoln wriggled from the moment he was born.

Like a tadpole, thought Abraham, and he called his son "Tad."

The name stuck.

So did the wriggle.

Born with an opening in the roof of his mouth, Tad baffled listeners with words that twisted and tumbled out of control. Few people understood him as he ran and jabbered and bubbled with ideas.

The President's House had never hosted the likes of Tad Lincoln.

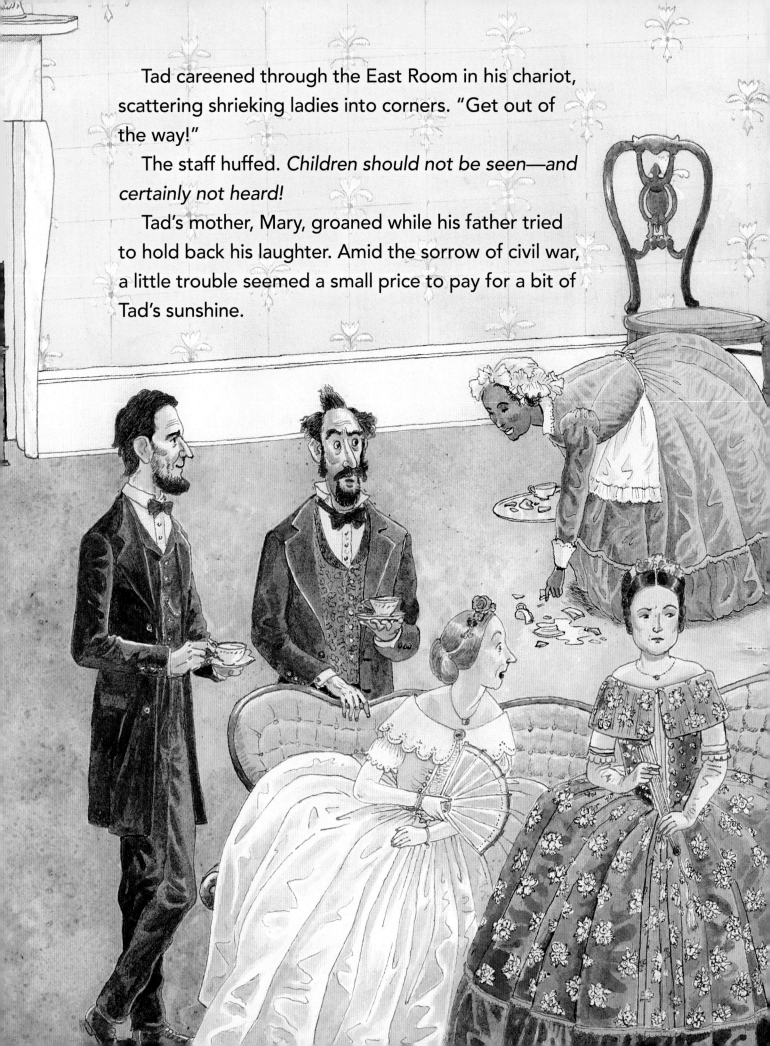

Tad careened through the East Room in his chariot, scattering shrieking ladies into corners. "Get out of the way!"

The staff huffed. *Children should not be seen—and certainly not heard!*

Tad's mother, Mary, groaned while his father tried to hold back his laughter. Amid the sorrow of civil war, a little trouble seemed a small price to pay for a bit of Tad's sunshine.

Tad seemed to be everywhere at once—everywhere except his classroom.

Tutor after tutor tried. *Letters have sounds!*

But letters didn't make sense to Tad. Lessons launched him down the hall and out the door.

"Let him run," said Papa.

Tad ran—from stable to portico . . .

attic to basement . . .

soldier's camp to . . .

BAM!

Tad burst through the door, leaped onto his father, squeeeeezed him with a wild hug, and scurried out.

Statesmen grumbled. *Couldn't he knock?*

Papa's eyes lit up as Tad's laughter faded down the hall.

Since the death of Tad's brother Willie a year ago, father and son needed each other more than ever.

Papa guided Tad's wriggle through the streets of
Washington. As his father attended to presidential
business, Tad watched and listened and learned.

At the telegraph office, Papa read messages from generals on battlefields.

At hospitals, he comforted wounded soldiers.

On the way home, Papa picked up stray kittens, chatted with storekeepers, and thanked volunteers raising money for bandages.

When Tad turned ten, the Lincoln family visited an army camp. They slept in tents, reviewed troops, and trotted across the countryside while cannons boomed in the distance.

Back home, Tad led his own troops—racing his pony across the lawn . . . chasing Nanny goat through flower beds . . . burying toy soldiers under rose bushes.

Papa chuckled, but the gardener raged. If the boy's father wouldn't do something, someone else would have to. That goat would have to go!

While Tad was away . . . Nanny disappeared.

In search of a new playmate, Tad surveyed the line of visitors waiting to see his father. Too many people! And Papa never turned anyone away.

Tad sprang into action! He questioned one person after another. People struggled to understand his jumbled words.

Women requested passes across enemy lines.
Families begged for money.
Politicians wanted favors.

Like his father, Tad listened to each one's story. Though he couldn't read books, he could read people. He sent the greedy home and took the most deserving upstairs. Papa smiled.

But when generals appealed for bandages and medicine, Papa's shoulders slumped lower, and his face sagged sadder.

Tad's brain wriggled with ideas to raise money.
Though numbers on a slate confused him, Tad
understood business.

He charged five-cent tolls at the stairway.

Until Papa opened the gate.

Tad sold apples, jerky, and broken toys.
Until Papa asked him to close.

Tad raided his parents' wardrobes and held a yard sale.
Until Papa dashed out to save his suits.
But Tad had seen a twinkle in Papa's eyes . . .

So he kept trying.
Retreating to Papa's office, Tad offered a pen
for presidential notes and kept his father company
while he worked.

Long about midnight, Papa scooped up his son
and carried him to bed.

Papa guided Tad's wriggle into the streets of Washington. As his son delivered special messages on his own, Papa watched the restless wriggle settle into Tad's heart.

On the way to the War Department, Tad cheered the soldiers.

On the way to the fire department, he gave coins to the homeless.

On the way home, Tad picked up stray dogs and rounded up street kids and marched them into the kitchen.

When the cook protested—
this was the President's House!—Tad
persisted. *But this was his home!*

And when a turkey arrived near the end of the year, Tad took charge.

He introduced "Jack" to his menagerie, and within days, the bird strutted after him like a new recruit.

The staff chuckled. The cook shook her head. She'd have to get that turkey back!

On Christmas Eve, Jack disappeared.

Tad raced—

from stable

to portico . . .

attic to basement . . .

soldiers' camp to . . .

SQUAWK!

Tad burst into the kitchen. There was Jack—with the cook!

Tad scrambled up the stairs and barged into his father's office. His words gushed and tumbled, pleading for Jack, proclaiming his goodness.

Papa understood. He scribbled an official note excusing Jack from dinner.

Tad grabbed the paper and rushed off to rescue his pet.

With Jack safe, Tad sorted through his presents.
Papa would never have time to read all these books
to him.

Suddenly, his eyes lit up. Books! For soldiers in the
hospital!

Arms loaded, he hurried to Papa's office to share his plan.

Papa grinned and drew Tad close. "Yes, my son, send a big box. Ask Mother for plenty of warm things . . . pack in all the good eatables."

Tad dashed from bedrooms to kitchen to pantry. He commandeered blankets and socks and treats. He jabbered and shrieked as he piled up gifts for the soldiers.

Though Tad couldn't write a note himself, his message was clear as he filled the very big box . . .

. . . with love,
and comfort,
and a wriggle of sunshine!

Love is the chain whereby to bind a child to its parents.

—Abraham Lincoln

AUTHOR'S NOTE

What began as the tale of the first presidential turkey pardon quickly led to a deeper story of the love between a father and son. In 1863, the nation was in the middle of the Civil War, and the Lincoln family was in the middle of their own deep sadness after the death of Tad's brother Willie, a year earlier. As I learned about this special father and son relationship, it touched me to see how Abraham guided Tad with love and patience, and how Tad cheered up Abraham with his boisterous energy and generous spirit. Tad and Abraham had very different personalities but were bound by their love for animals, lively sense of humor, and endless compassion for others. Tad's pure heart and the goodness of children gave Abraham hope for the future.

This story focuses on Tad Lincoln's life during the year 1863.

MORE ABOUT TAD AND THE LINCOLNS

The Lincoln family moved from Illinois to Washington, DC, in February 1861 when Tad was almost eight years old. After the presidential inauguration, Tad's oldest brother Robert returned to college, and Willie (age ten) and Tad settled into the President's House. A year later, Willie and Tad became very sick. Tad recovered, but Willie did not.

Life in the President's House during wartime was challenging. But Tad had additional problems. Photographs of Tad and historical evidence on his speech habits, pronunciation, crooked teeth, and need for specially prepared food show that it was most likely a partial cleft palate that caused the small opening in the roof of his mouth. Today, surgeons can repair this birth defect, but in Tad's time, that wasn't possible. Because he couldn't pronounce some sounds and his words "flooded" out, few people could understand him, and kids often made fun of him. Tad also appears to have had a language-based learning disability. Frequent illness, traveling, and being in the busy President's House created even more challenges, making lessons very frustrating for Tad. Despite his speech and learning difficulties, he showed wisdom beyond his years.

Abraham and Mary Lincoln were not like other parents of the time. Many people criticized them for not making Tad do his schoolwork or behave appropriately. But it's clear that Abraham needed Tad's sunshine just as much as Tad needed Abraham's patience.

In 1865, after Abraham Lincoln was assassinated, Mary and Tad left the President's House. Tad realized it was time to grow up. He studied with tutors in Chicago, and then in Germany, and learned to speak clearly, read, and write. On their return trip to Chicago, he became ill, and in 1871, at the age of eighteen, Tad died.

THE TRADITION OF THE PRESIDENTIAL TURKEY PARDON

The President of the United States has the power to forgive a person for a crime or to excuse a person from punishment. This idea was humorously extended to presidential turkeys.

In Lincoln's time and beyond, turkey farmers often provided birds for the First Family's holiday meals. In 1947, the poultry industry made the gift of a Thanksgiving turkey an official tradition, and through the years presidents often sent the turkeys to a farm or zoo. But it was George H. W. Bush who first used the term "presidential pardon" for turkeys in 1989. Since then, every White House Thanksgiving turkey has received a pardon. Although it took many years to become official, Abraham Lincoln was the first to allow a presidential holiday turkey to escape the dinner table, all because of Tad's generous heart.

TAD IN PICTURES

LITTLE "TAD" LINCOLN.

Father and son in 1865, the final year of the Civil War

Young Tad in uniform, ready to lead his troops

Tad rode his pony on the grounds of the President's House and at army camps. He also served as an escort when his parents took carriage rides.

A Currier & Ives print of the Lincoln family: Mary, Robert, Tad, and Abraham

THE LINCOLN FAMILY.

BIBLIOGRAPHY

PRIMARY SOURCES

Bates, David Homer. "Lincoln's Love for His Children." In *Lincoln in the Telegraph Office: Recollections of the United States Military Telegraph Corps During the Civil War*, 208–27. New York: The Century Co., 1907.

Bayne, Julia Taft. *Tad Lincoln's Father*. Lincoln: University of Nebraska Press, 2001.

Brooks, Noah. "A Boy in the White House." *St. Nicholas: A Monthly Magazine for Boys and Girls*, vol. 10, November 1882, 57–65.

———. *Lincoln Observed: Civil War Dispatches of Noah Brooks*. Edited by Michael Burlingame. Baltimore: Johns Hopkins University Press, 1998.

———. "Personal Reminiscences of Lincoln." *Scribner's Monthly: An Illustrated Magazine for the People*, vol. 15, no. 5, March 1878, 673–81.

Carpenter, F. B. *Six Months at the White House with Abraham Lincoln*. New York: Hurd & Houghton, 1866.

Crook, W. H. *Memories of the White House: The Home Life of Our Presidents from Lincoln to Roosevelt*. Edited by Henry Rood. Boston: Little, Brown, 1911.

Helm, Katherine. *The True Story of Mary, Wife of Lincoln: Containing the Recollections of Mary Lincoln's Sister Emilie (Mrs. Ben Hardin Helm), Extracts from Her War-Time Diary, Numerous Letters and Other Documents Now First Published by Her Niece, Katherine Helm*. New York: Harper, 1928.

Keckley, Elizabeth. *Behind the Scenes, or, Thirty Years a Slave, and Four Years in the White House*. New York: G. W. Carleton & Co., 1868.

Pendel, Thomas. *Thirty-Six Years in the White House, by Thomas F. Pendel, Door-Keeper; Lincoln-Roosevelt*. Washington: The Neale Publishing Company, 1902.

Stoddard, William O. *Inside the White House in War Times: Memoirs and Reports of Lincoln's Secretary*. Edited by Michael Burlingame. Lincoln: University of Nebraska Press, 2000.

SECONDARY SOURCES

Brown, R. J. "Tad Lincoln: The Not-So-Famous Son of a Most-Famous President." HistoryBuff.com. web.archive.org/web/20160304130505/http://www.historyreference.org/library/reftad.html.

Burlingame, Michael. *The Inner World of Abraham Lincoln*. Urbana: University of Illinois Press, 1997.

The Gilder Lehrman Institute of American History. Mr. Lincoln's White House. mrlincolnswhitehouse.org/.

Hutchinson, John M. "What Was Tad Lincoln's Speech Problem?" *Journal of the Abraham Lincoln Association* 30, no. 1 (Winter 2009): 35–51.

King, Gilbert. "The History of Pardoning Turkeys Began With Tad Lincoln." *Smithsonian*. November 21, 2012. smithsonianmag.com/history/the-history-of-pardoning-turkeys-began-with-tad-lincoln-141137570/.

Klein, Christopher. "A Brief History of the Presidential Turkey Pardon." History. November 25, 2014. history.com/news/a-brief-history-of-the-presidential-turkey-pardon.

Manning, Alan. *Father Lincoln: The Untold Story of Abraham Lincoln and His Boys—Robert, Eddy, Willie, and Tad*. Guilford, CT: Lyons Press, 2016.

Monkman, Betty C. "Pardoning the Thanksgiving Turkey." The White House Historical Association. whitehousehistory.org/pardoning-the-thanksgiving-turkey.

Morrison, James, and Kathryn Flegel. *Interviewing Children and Adolescents, Second Edition: Skills and Strategies for Effective DSM-5® Diagnosis*. 2nd ed., 200–201. New York: Guilford Publications, 2016.

National Constitution Center. "The Real Story behind the Presidential Turkey Pardon." *Constitution Daily* (blog). November 21, 2017. constitutioncenter.org/blog/the-real-story-behind-the-presidential-turkey-pardon.

Norton, R. J. "Tad Lincoln." Abraham Lincoln Research Site. rogerjnorton.com/Lincoln69.html.

———. "Tad Lincoln Saves Jack." Abraham Lincoln Research Site. rogerjnorton.com/Lincoln65.html.

Pinsker, Matthew. *Lincoln's Sanctuary: Abraham Lincoln and the Soldiers' Home*. Oxford: Oxford University Press, 2003.

Randall, Ruth Painter. *Lincoln's Sons*. Boston: Little, Brown and Company, 1955.

———. *Mary Lincoln Biography of a Marriage*. Boston: Little Brown, 1953.

Sweetser, Kate Dickinson. "Tyrant Tad: The Boy in the White House." In *Ten Boys from History*, 145–68. New York: Harper & Brothers, 1910.

Truman, Margaret. "The Lincoln Pets." In *White House Pets*, 54–64. Philadelphia: D. McKay Co., 1969.

Washington, John E. *They Knew Lincoln*. Boston: E. P. Dutton & Co., 1942.

Watson, Robert P., and Dale Berger. "Lincoln's Boys: The Legacy of an American Father and an American Family." *AMERICANA e-Journal of American Studies in Hungary* 6, no. 1 (spring 2010).

Weaver, John D. *Tad Lincoln: Mischief-Maker in the White House*. New York: Dodd, Mead, 1963.

Whitcomb, John, and Claire Whitcomb. "Abraham Lincoln, 1861–April 14, 1865: A 'Whited Sepulcure.'" In *Real Life at the White House: Two Hundred Years of Daily Life at America's Most Famous Residence*, 129–42. New York: Routledge, 2000.

The White House. "The Grounds: The White House Building." whitehouse.gov/about-the-white-house/the-white-house/.

SOURCE NOTES

"Get out of the way!" Brooks, *A Boy in the White House*, p. 58.
"Let him run." Brooks, *A Boy in the White House*, p. 61.
"Yes, my son, send . . ." Randall, *Lincoln's Sons*, p. 131.
"Love is the chain . . ." Randall, *Mary Lincoln Biography of a Marriage*, p. 101.
"I don't know but I may succeed . . ." Burlingame, *The Inner World of Abraham Lincoln*, p. 67.

ACKNOWLEDGMENTS

Immense thanks to Michelle Krowl and Edith Sandler at the amazing Library of Congress; to James M. Cornelius, PhD, Editor and Historian for the Abraham Lincoln Association; and to my critique partners for all their valuable feedback. Continuing appreciation to my agent, Stephanie Fretwell-Hill, and to Carolyn Yoder, editor extraordinaire, for believing in my storytelling. And eternal gratitude to my family for their support and inspiration.

PICTURE CREDITS

Library of Congress Prints and Photographs Division, LC-USZ62-7990: 37 (top, left); LC-DIG-ppmsca-19225: 37 (bottom, left); LC-USZ62-8262: 37 (top, right); LC-DIG-pga-09298: 37 (bottom, right).

To my parents, who will forever be my models for living —*BA*

To Mark, also once quite a wriggler —*SDS*

Text copyright © 2021 by Beth Anderson
Illustrations copyright © 2021 by S. D. Schindler
All rights reserved. Copying or digitizing this book for storage,
display, or distribution in any other medium is strictly prohibited.

For information about permission to reproduce selections from
this book, please contact permissions@bmkbooks.com.

Calkins Creek
An imprint of Boyds Mills & Kane, a division of Astra Publishing House
calkinscreekbooks.com
Printed in China

ISBN: 978-1-63592-315-5 (hc)
ISBN: 978-1-63592-462-6 (eBook)
Library of Congress Control Number: 2020947820

First edition
10 9 8 7 6 5 4 3 2 1

Design by Barbara Grzeslo
The type is set in Avenir Std.
The illustrations are done in India ink, transparent inks, watercolor, and gouache.